20.99

Fort Lupton Public & School Library
425 South Denver Avenue
Fort Lupton, CO 80621
fortluptonlibrary.org
303-857-7180

D0463143

Hawai'i

THE ALOHA STATE

www.av2books.com

MEDIA ENHANCED BOOKS
AV²
BY WEIGL™
ADDED VALUE • AUDIO VISUAL

AV² provides enriched content that supplements and complements this book. Weigl's AV² books strive to create inspired learning and engage young minds in a total learning experience.

Your AV² Media Enhanced books come alive with...

 Audio
Listen to sections of the book read aloud.

 **Key Words**
Study vocabulary, and complete a matching word activity.

 Video
Watch informative video clips.

Quizzes
Test your knowledge.

 **Embedded Weblinks**
Gain additional information for research.

 Slide Show
View images and captions, and prepare a presentation.

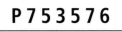 **Try This!**
Complete activities and hands-on experiments.

... and much, much more!

Go to **www.av2books.com**, and enter this book's unique code.

BOOK CODE

P 7 5 3 5 7 6

AV² by Weigl brings you media enhanced books that support active learning.

Published by AV² by Weigl
350 5th Avenue, 59th Floor
New York, NY 10118
Website: www.av2books.com   www.weigl.com

Copyright 2012 AV² by Weigl
All rights reserved. No part of this publication may be reproduced, stored in a retrieval system, or transmitted in any form or by any means, electronic, mechanical, photocopying, recording, or otherwise, without the prior written permission of the publisher.

Library of Congress Cataloging-in-Publication Data

Foran, Jill.
 Hawai'i / Jill Foran.
    p. cm. -- (A guide to American states)
 Includes index.
 ISBN 978-1-61690-783-9 (hardcover : alk. paper) -- ISBN 978-1-61690-459-3 (online)
 1. Hawaii--Juvenile literature. I. Title. II. Title: Hawaii.
 DU623.25.F675 2011
 996.9--dc23
                        2011018323

Printed in the United States of America in North Mankato, Minnesota

052011
WEP180511

Project Coordinator Jordan McGill
Art Director Terry Paulhus

Photo Credits
Every reasonable effort has been made to trace ownership and to obtain permission to reprint copyright material. The publishers would be pleased to have any errors or omissions brought to their attention so that they may be corrected in subsequent printings.

Weigl acknowledges Getty Images as its primary image supplier for this title.

Contents

The 80-foot high waterfalls of Rainbow Falls cascades down into a 100-foot-wide pool of turquoise water. Morning is the best time to visit this natural wonder on Hawai'i's Big Island. The morning sunlight on the rising water vapor creates a rainbow.

Introduction

Hawai'i, the 50th state in the Union, consists of a group of islands in the north central Pacific Ocean. It is unique among the states in that it is the only one made up entirely of islands. It is also the only state in which the majority of the population does not trace its heritage back to Europe.

Hawai'i has been nicknamed the Aloha State. Aloha is a Hawai'ian word with many meanings, among them "welcome," "love," "hello," and "goodbye." The word aloha reveals the warm and welcoming nature of the Hawai'ian people. Visitors from around the world come to Hawai'i to enjoy its tropical paradise.

Hawai'i's many beaches are enjoyed by locals and tourists alike. The warm ocean waters and mild climate make the beaches a popular place to relax.

More than 30 million passengers used Hawai'i's airports in 2009. For most tourists, air travel is the best way to reach Hawai'i.

Hawai'i lies almost entirely in the tropics. Separated from the U.S. mainland by thousands of miles of ocean, Hawai'i is the only state that does not fall within the continent of North America. It holds a strategic position in the defense of the United States. Pearl Harbor, a vast shipyard for the repair and overhaul of U.S. fleet units, is the home port for many U.S. naval ships. It serves as a training base for submarine-warfare and antisubmarine forces.

Hawai'i has no immediate neighbors. These distances do not stop millions of visitors from coming to the Aloha State every year. Driving to the islands from the mainland is not possible, but many airlines offer regular flights to Hawai'i. Hawai'i has nine commercial airports to accommodate the large number of flights. You can also take a boat to Hawai'i. Cruise ships and other boats frequent the waters surrounding the islands.

Where Is Hawai'i?

Hawai'i is completely surrounded by the Pacific Ocean. It is the most isolated population center in the world. It is 2,390 miles from California; 3,850 miles from Japan; 4,900 miles from China; and 5,280 miles from the Philippines.

Hawai'i is made up of eight main islands. They are Hawai'i, Maui, Molokai, Lanai, Oahu, Kauai, Niihau, and Kahoolawe. Hawai'i also includes 124 **islets**. The island of Hawai'i is nicknamed the Big Island because it is by far the largest island. It is best known for its volcanoes. Much of the island is covered in volcanic ash and lava beds. Maui is nicknamed the Valley Isle because its two volcanic mountains are separated by lush land. Maui's rich red soil lines the roads and provides great land for farming. The Friendly Isle, Molokai, is known for its friendly people. Each region on the island is very different. One region has mountains and high cliffs, and another has dry land used mainly for cattle ranching. The last region is covered with pineapple plantations.

Kilauea is the most active volcano on Earth. Located in Hawai'i Volcanoes National Park, it has added 300 acres of coastal land to the island since 1983.

Lanai is called the Private Island because few tourists know they can visit it. Oahu, called the Gathering Place, is the most populated island. Pearl Harbor is on Oahu's southern coast. Honolulu, the state's capital, is also on Oahu. Kauai is nicknamed the Garden Isle because of its lush green vegetation and its many streams and waterfalls. Kauai receives more rain than any of the other islands. The rain has worn away much of the land and carved out Kauai's steep canyons and cliffs. Niihau is called the Forbidden Island because the public cannot visit it. Niihau is private property. A woman named Elizabeth Sinclair bought the island in 1864. Her descendants now live there and operate a cattle ranch that covers almost the entire island. Kahoolawe does not have a nickname. No one lives there. It is the smallest of the islands, and its land cannot support many crops.

I DIDN'T KNOW THAT!

Hawai'i was the last state to enter the Union.

Hawai'i's islands are almost all volcanic in origin. Hawai'i has the world's largest active and largest inactive volcanoes.

Lanai was once owned by the Dole Food Company. It used to be known as Pineapple Island.

Because of its location in the Pacific Ocean, Hawai'i has great strategic value for the United States. Pearl Harbor on Oahu remains a massive military base and port.

Mapping Hawai'i

Hawai'i is located in the North Pacific Ocean. Its principal islands are just a few degrees south of the Tropic of Cancer. It is in the Hawai'i-Aleutian time zone, which is 2 hours earlier than the Pacific time zone. Because of its isolated location, Hawai'i is not considered a part of the continent of North America.

Sites and Symbols

STATE SEAL
Hawai'i

STATE BIRD
Nene
(Hawai'ian Goose)

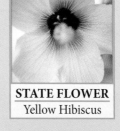

STATE FLOWER
Yellow Hibiscus

STATE FLAG
Hawai'i

STATE MAMMAL
Hawai'ian Monk Seal

STATE TREE
Kukui (Candlenut)

Nickname The Aloha State

Motto *Ua Mau ke Ea o ka Aina i ka Pono* (The Life of the Land Is Perpetuated in Righteousness)

Song "Hawai'i Ponoi" (Hawai'i's Own) by King David Kalakaua and Henri Berger

Entered the Union August 21, 1959, as the 50th state

Capital Honolulu

Population (2010 Census) 1,360,301

Ranked 40th state

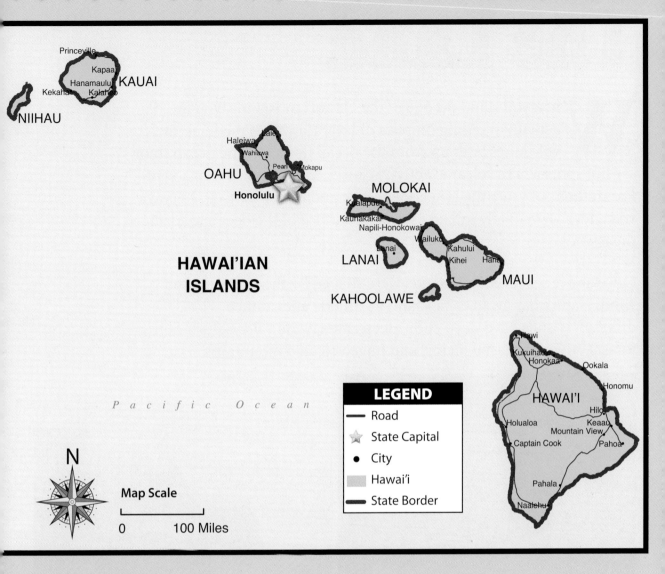

Princeville
Kapaa
Hanamaulu **KAUAI**
Kekaha
Kalaheo

NIIHAU

Haleiwa
Wahiawa
OAHU
Pearl Mokapu
Honolulu

MOLOKAI
Kualapuu
Kaunakakai
Napili-Honokowai
Wailuku
Kahului
Lanai
Kihei
Hana

LANAI

**HAWAI'IAN
ISLANDS**

MAUI

KAHOOLAWE

P a c i f i c   O c e a n

Hawi
Kukuihaele
Honokaa
Ookala
Honomu
HAWAI'I
Holualoa
Hilo
Keaau
Mountain View
Captain Cook
Pahoa
Pahala
Naalehu

N

Map Scale

0   100 Miles

LEGEND

——	Road
⭐	State Capital
●	City
▨	Hawai'i
▬	State Border

STATE
CAPITAL

Honolulu, Hawai'i's capital, is
located on the island of Oahu. No
one knows for certain when it was
founded, but archaeologists date it to at least
1100 AD The word Honolulu means "sheltered
harbor," and it is Honolulu's deep harbor that has
made it a favorable place to trade and settle.
About 375,000 people live in the
city of Honolulu.

United States

Hawai'i   Alaska

The Land

When you stand on one of the Hawai'ian Islands, you are actually standing on piles of lava. Hawai'i is made up of volcanoes built up from the ocean floor. On the ocean floor are hot spots where volcanic activity causes lava to flow out of a vent. For millions of years the lava added layer upon layer to itself. Massive volcanoes were finally forced above the surface of the ocean to form the islands.

Once above sea level, the islands were shaped by the sea, rain, and wind. Nature has given each island its unique appearance. The different islands have steep cliffs, deep caves, wide valleys, lush rain forests, miles of coastal plains, and huge volcanic mountains.

FERN FORESTS

Rich soil from ancient volcanoes makes possible the growth of lush fern forests in parts of Hawai'i.

SEACLIFFS

Hawai'i's breathtaking sea cliffs are the result of ocean waves pounding against hills formed by the lava flow of volcanoes.

DIAMOND HEAD

Diamond Head, on Oahu, was named by early explorers who thought the glittering face of this Hawai'ian mountain actually contained diamonds.

BEACHES

Erosion and rising sea levels have swallowed part of some Hawai'ian beaches. Recently, sand has been pumped from areas of the ocean floor to fill in shrinking beaches.

The Big Island of Hawai'i has two active volcanoes, Mauna Loa and Kilauea.

Mauna Loa is the largest volcano on Earth. Its size is about 19,000 cubic miles.

Mount Waialeale on the island of Kauai is one of the wettest spots in the world. The average annual rainfall is about 450 inches.

Hawai'i temperatures stay fairly constant all year round, making it a popular vacation playground.

Climate

Trade winds keep Hawai'i's mild climate agreeable year-round. Winter temperatures barely differ from summer temperatures. In fact, temperatures range between about 72° and 79° Fahrenheit throughout the year. Temperatures in the mountains are cooler, and winter snow sometimes blankets the tops of Mauna Kea and Mauna Loa.

Most Hawai'ians recognize only two seasons. Summer lasts from May through October, and winter lasts from November to April.

Average Annual Precipitation Across Hawai'i

There is a great deal of variation in the amount of rainfall that different locations in Hawai'i receive. What do you think might account for these differences?

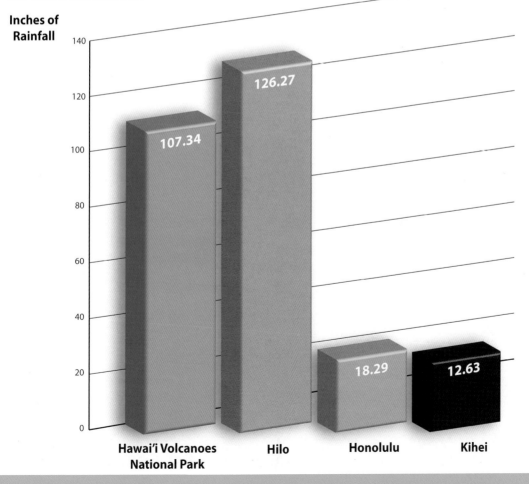

Natural Resources

Imagine having a shortage of water when you are surrounded by the Pacific Ocean. Hawai'ians have access to all the salt water they want, but when it comes to freshwater, their supply is limited. There are a number of streams, ponds, and waterfalls on the islands, but there are no big lakes to supply freshwater. Hawai'ians depend on rainfall for much of their freshwater. Rain seeps through the rocky surface of the land and creates large underground reserves of freshwater. Thick clusters of tropical plants and trees grow in areas where the rainfall is heaviest.

Sugar cane grows in the fields of Maui. The cane is harvested and processed into sugar, most of which is then shipped to the U. S. mainland for consumption.

Hawai'i's soil is good for growing tropical fruits and plants. Sugarcane and pineapples are the most important crops on the islands. They are key contributors to Hawai'i's economy. The land is also good for growing macadamia nuts, coffee, and such fruits as guavas, mangoes, and papayas.

Hawai'i must import oil for most of its energy needs, but Hawai'ians have been exploring alternative sources of energy, too. Several islands generate their own hydroelectric power. A **geothermal** plant produces about one-fifth of the electricity for the island of Hawai'i. The Kaheawa wind farm began operating on Maui in 2006.

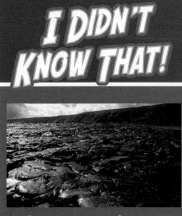

Only 8 percent of Hawai'i's land is used for crops. There are huge areas of barren lava rock where soil is weak or nonexistent.

Hawai'i has no important mineral or oil deposits. Most mining is limited to recovering crushed stone and cement. Stone and cement are important for building roads.

Wind energy is a source of electricity in Hawai'i because of the trade winds.

An estimated 80,000 single-family homes, multi-unit dwellings, and institutional facilities in Hawai'i are served by solar water heaters.

Hawai'i has been experimenting with the use of PowerBuoys that collect energy from ocean waves. The energy is transformed into electricity.

Kona coffee, for which Hawaii is famous, requires high elevation, rich volcanic soil, seasonal rainfall, and afternoon cloud cover to produce its distinct flavor.

Plants

Many plants grew in Hawai'i long before human settlers arrived. Seeds carried by birds, wind, and ocean tides likely caused the early plant life to flourish. Settlers later introduced new plants to Hawai'i. Polynesian settlers brought edible plants such as coconut, **taro**, banana, and sugarcane. They also brought the kukui tree, which is the state tree. Later, settlers introduced many exotic flowers.

Hawai'i's environment is very delicate. The main islands are slowly being worn down. Nature's elements are gradually eroding the volcanic mountains. People contribute to the damage by overusing the land. Hawai'ians are aware of their fragile surroundings and are now taking measures to protect their land.

State and national parks help prevent further damage caused by humans. Hawai'i has more than 50 state parks and two important national parks.

ANTHURIUM

Anthuriums are just one of the many beautiful tropical flowers growing in Hawai'i. Over 12 million anthuriums are shipped from Hawai'i every year.

PLUMERIA

Plumeria is the most common flower to be found in Hawaii. It is used in most leis that are given to visitors as they arrive on the islands.

COCONUT PALM

Coconut palm trees are one of the varieties of palm commonly found in Hawai'i. The coconut fruit comes from this tree.

FERNS

Ferns make their home in the crevasses of lava that has cooled over a period of years and has begun to break down into soil.

The kukui, or candlenut, tree was very useful to early Hawai'ians. The kukui nut provided oil for lamps and medicine for sealing cuts. While fishing, Hawai'ians would spit chewed kukui kernels into the ocean, which they believed would calm the waters.

Plants and flowers are in bloom all year on the islands.

There are more than 5,000 varieties of the hibiscus flower in Hawai'i.

Animals

There are very few land animals in Hawai'i that are native to the islands. Only land snails, insects, a rare bat species, and a number of birds can claim native status. Human settlers brought all of Hawai'i's other animals to the islands. These included dogs, cats, horses, cows, goats, pigs, reptiles, and amphibians.

Life in the ocean is much more diverse than on land. Several hundred species of fish swim in Hawai'ian waters. About one-third of these species can be found only in Hawai'i. The fish share their waters with dolphins, sharks, humpback whales, and sea turtles.

GOAT

Goats that overgraze Hawai'i's fields are responsible for the erosion of soil in some places. Goat are not native to Hawai'i but were brought in by settlers.

HUMPBACK WHALE

The humpback whale is known for its breaching, when it lifts nearly two thirds of its body out of the water. Researchers think the whales breach as part of their playing.

PARROT

People imported parrots to the Hawai'ian Islands. Today, many parrots are pets but some live in the wild.

RACCOON BUTTERFLYFISH

The raccoon butterflyfish is one of the many varieties of tropical fish living in and around Hawai'i's reefs. At night, or when frightened, this fish's body turns darker in color and takes on a blotchy appearance.

Wild animals in Hawai'i are usually domesticated stock gone astray. Wild pigs and goats have done a lot of damage to vegetation and soil.

Hawai'i's unofficial state fish is the humuhumunukunuku apua'a. It is also known as the rectangular triggerfish.

About one third of all the animal species in the United States that are **threatened** or **endangered** are found in Hawai'i. The Hawai'i monk seal, which is the state mammal, is an endangered species.

Tourism

The beauty and attractions of the Hawai'ian Islands draw millions of visitors each year. At Diamond Head or Punchbowl, both in Honolulu, tourists can see the remnants of extinct volcanic vents. The USS *Arizona* Memorial, also in Honolulu, is a tribute to U.S. soldiers who died in the attack on Pearl Harbor. Other interesting sites for tourists are the royal Iolani Palace and the Polynesian Cultural Center. At the cultural center, visitors can walk around replicas of Polynesian villages.

The beaches are probably the main attraction for many visitors. The islands have miles of white sand beaches. Honolulu's Waikiki Beach is one of the most famous beaches in the world. It offers just about any water sport, beachfront shops, and plenty of sunshine. Other beaches in the state are equally appealing. The beautiful black sand beaches on the Big Island are also popular tourist spots.

WAIKIKI BEACH

Waikiki Beach, on the south shore of Oahu, is the most-developed tourist area in Hawai'i. Located just below Diamond Head, the beach is two miles long.

GOLF COURSES

Many of the dozens of golf courses in Hawai'i are championship golf courses. Professional tournaments played on these courses bring many visitors to the state.

USS *ARIZONA* MEMORIAL

The USS *Arizona* Memorial honors those who died at Pearl Harbor in the Japanese attack on December 7, 1941. In the shrine room of the 184-foot-long Memorial structure is a wall engraved with the names of the men killed on the ship that day.

POLYNESIAN CULTURAL CENTER

The Polynesian Cultural Center is a living museum located on Oahu. In villages based on traditional Polynesian life, performers demonstrate various arts and crafts, including dancing. The center also offers shows and canoe rides in a lagoon.

I DIDN'T KNOW THAT!

Honolulu alone has more than 50 miles of beaches.

The sand on the Big Island is black because of bits of lava from volcanic eruptions that have eroded and mixed with sand.

Most of Hawai'i's visitors come from the U.S. mainland, Canada, Australia, and countries in Asia, especially Japan.

Industry

Tourism is Hawai'i's most successful industry. Almost 7 million tourists visit the state each year. Another leading source of income in Hawai'i is food processing. Sugarcane is processed into raw sugar or molasses and is then sent to the mainland. Similarly, pineapple is canned, frozen, or juiced and then sold on the mainland. Tropical fruits, such as guavas and papayas, are often processed into jams and jellies.

Industries in Hawai'i
Value of Goods and Services in Millions of Dollars

The pie chart below shows how important different industries are to Hawai'i. Why is mining such a small part of Hawai'i's value of goods and services?

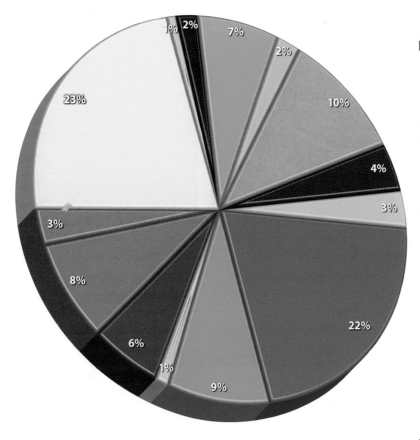

LEGEND

Agriculture, Forestry, and Fishing	$422
* Mining	$22
Utilities	$1,493
Construction	$4,443
Manufacturing	$1,298
Wholesale and Retail Trade	$6,594
Transportation	$2,389
Media and Entertainment	$2,231
Finance, Insurance, and Real Estate	$14,799
Professional and Technical Services	$5,897
Education	$671
Health Care	$3,967
Hotels and Restaurants	$5,210
Other Services	$1,776
Government	$14,927
TOTAL	**$66,139**

*Less than 1%. Percentages may not add to 100 because of rounding.

Hawai'i's warm climate makes it an ideal place to grow tropical fruits. More acreage is planted in pineapples than in any other fruit.

I DIDN'T KNOW THAT!

The first successful sugarcane plantation in Hawai'i was established in 1835. Soon after, pioneers began moving to Hawai'i to grow sugarcane.

The first successful flight between the mainland and Hawai'i was in 1927. Two Army lieutenants flew from Oakland, California, to Oahu in 25 hours and 50 minutes. Air travel opened up a world of opportunity for Hawai'i's tourist industry.

Military personnel and their families account for about 80,000 of the people living in Hawai'i.

Hawai'ian papayas weigh about 1 pound each. The plants grow no more than 8 feet tall.

Hawai'i is the only state in which coffee is grown.

Goods and Services

Hawai'i is very isolated from the rest of the United States, so it is completely dependent on sea and air transportation for its economic growth. Ships carry and deliver most of the food, consumer goods, and raw materials used in Hawai'i. Imported consumer products add to the high cost of living on the islands. Everything is more expensive because it is harder to get.

Despite the reliance on imports, Hawai'i does export some products. The state's leading exports are raw sugar, molasses, pineapples, clothing, flowers, and cement.

About 98 percent of Hawai'i's imports are brought in by ship.

The islands are not only isolated from the mainland, they are also isolated from one another. Transportation is difficult because the islands are so far apart. There is air travel between the islands so that visitors and Hawai'ians alike can quickly get to other parts of the state. Hawai'i has several airports to accommodate the air traffic.

The University of Hawai'i is based in Honolulu, but it also has campuses on other islands. Several community colleges are also spread out among the islands.

The state is served by a single library system, which includes 51 branches on six islands.

About one out of every four workers in Hawai'i belongs to a union, making Hawai'i one of the most unionized states in the United States.

The north shore of Kauai was once the site of a famous hula school. Chanters would stand at the edge of the sea and test their voices against the crashing of the waves.

The beautiful printed fabric of Hawai'ian shirts makes them popular wear for men, women, and children.

Native Hawai'ians

The first people to set foot on the Hawai'ian Islands were Polynesian voyagers. Perhaps as early as AD 400 these voyagers left their homes on other Pacific islands and sailed in canoes to the Hawai'ian Islands. They named the area Hawai'i.

There are two theories about the naming of the islands. Many people believe that the Polynesian chief Hawai'i Loa discovered the islands. The settlers may have named Hawai'i after him. However, it is also possible that the islands were named after Hawaiki, which is the name of the traditional Polynesian homeland.

Native Hawai'ians had been living undisturbed for hundreds of years before Captain James Cook visited the islands in the late 1700s.

After the initial discovery of the Hawai'ian Islands, waves of Polynesian immigrants, mostly from the island of Tahiti, moved to Hawai'i. The islands were divided into several kingdoms, each ruled by a separate chief. These kingdoms were often at war with one another. The people were not united. This lack of unity made it possible for Europeans and Americans to convince Hawai'ians to abandon their culture.

Native Hawai'ians were highly skilled fishers and farmers. They lived in a complex society with laws set down by chiefs and priests. They believed in a group of gods who controlled the world but who also could come to Earth and interact with humans.

When Polynesian settlers came to Hawai'i, they cleared the land to grow taro, sweet potato, banana, and other plants. They often shared food from the same pot.

I DIDN'T KNOW THAT!

Native Hawai'ians came from parts of Polynesia, island groups in the central and southern regions of the Pacific Ocean.

It is believed that Polynesians from the Marquesas Islands were the first to discover Hawai'i. People from Tahiti came to Hawai'i afterward.

The first inhabitants of Hawai'i lived unobserved by the rest of the world for hundreds of years.

In Hawai'ian tradition, the Northwestern Hawai'ian Islands are considered a sacred place, from which life springs. The remote islands are home to many unusual sea animals, such as the hairy hermit crab.

When Captain Cook first came to the Hawai'ian Islands, the native Hawai'ians greeted him with hospitality.

Explorers and Missionaries

The Hawai'ian Islands remained unknown to most of the world until the late 1700s. In 1778, Captain James Cook of Great Britain and the members of his expedition became the first Europeans to see the islands. Soon after Cook's voyage, traders and explorers began to arrive. Hawai'i became an important port for European and North American ships that were on their way to trade their goods in East Asia. Foreign ships would remain in Hawai'ian harbors for months.

Local chiefs still ruled the islands at the time of Cook's discovery. In 1782 a chief named Kamehameha began a war against other chiefs in an attempt to gain control of all the islands. By 1810 Kamehameha had captured and unified the Hawai'ian Islands. His success was due largely to the firearms he obtained from traders and explorers who stopped at his port. Kamehameha became King Kamehameha I, the first ruler of unified Hawai'i.

Timeline of Settlement

Early Exploration

1778 The British explorer Captain James Cook reaches the Hawai'ian Islands.

1792 Captain George Vancouver brings livestock to the islands.

Hawai'ian Monarchy

1810 King Kamehameha I unites the islands and forms a **monarchy**.

1820 New England missionaries, led by Hiram Bingham, begin to arrive on the islands.

1848 The white minority convinces King Kamehameha III to accept the Great Mahele, or division of lands, which guarantees private ownership of property.

1875 The Reciprocity Treaty is a free trade agreement between Hawai'i and the United States.

1893 American and European businessmen overthrow the Hawai'ian monarchy.

United States Territory

1898 Hawai'i is annexed by the United States.

1900 Hawai'i becomes a U.S. territory.

1941 Japan bombs United States warships in Pearl Harbor, causing the United States to enter World War II.

Statehood

1959 Hawai'i becomes the 50th state, during President Dwight Eisenhower's administration.

Early Settlers

U nder King Kamehameha's rule, foreigners introduced cattle, horses, and many kinds of plants to the native Hawai'ians. They also introduced a number of infectious diseases. The Hawai'ian people had lived in isolation for many years and did not have the **immunities** to fight these diseases. Many of them died.

Map of Settlements and Resources in Early Hawai'i

❶ *Trade in **sandalwood** begins in Honolulu in 1805. The sandalwood is shipped to China, and all the sandalwood is harvested in a few decades.*

❺ *James Dole begins the commercial growing of pineapples in Wahaiwa in 1901.*

❻ *In 1922 Dole buys the island of Lanai and converts it into a pineapple plantation.*

❷ *In the 1820s Lahaina becomes a port for the whaling industry in the north-central Pacific Ocean.*

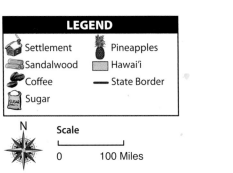

❸ *The growing of coffee is started in Kona and Hilo in 1829.*

❹ *In 1835, the first **viable** sugar plantation is started in Kauai.*

LEGEND

Settlement		Pineapples	
Sandalwood		Hawai'i	
Coffee		State Border	
Sugar			

N

Scale

0   100 Miles

When King Kamehameha I died in 1819, his son became his successor and took the name Kamehameha II. One of the king's first acts was to get rid of the local Hawai'ian religion. This religion included the belief in many gods and goddesses as well as human sacrifice.

Until 1848 the king owned all the land in Hawai'i. He granted or rented various areas to chiefs or to people from other countries. The new system introduced in 1848 divided the land and allowed commoners and foreigners to buy territory. The possibility of private ownership of Hawai'ian land encouraged foreigners to invest in the area.

Hawai'i's sugar industry took on huge economic importance once American investors could purchase Hawai'ian territory. The size and number of plantations grew. Soon there was a shortage of Hawai'ian workers for the fields. Plantation owners began to bring in laborers from China, Japan, the Philippines, Portugal, and other areas of the world. This contributed to the great cultural diversity that exists in Hawai'i today.

Desire for control of sugar production led American businessmen to overthrow the Hawai'ian monarchy and replace the government with a republic ruled by Americans.

In 1809 Kamehameha I established Honolulu as the capital of Hawai'i.

Hawai'i's population was estimated at 300,000 before explorers and traders arrived in the late 1700s. By 1820 the population of native inhabitants had fallen to just 135,000.

The British explorer James Cook named the Hawai'ian Islands the Sandwich Islands, in honor of his **patron**, the earl of Sandwich. The name did not stick.

When British explorers first arrived, the native Hawai'ians greeted them with open arms. However, in 1779 Captain Cook was killed in a fight between his crew and native Hawai'ians.

Hawai'i is the only U.S. state to have once been an independent monarchy.

Early American settlers came to Hawai'i because of the economic promise of the sugarcane industry. Most of this industry was introduced under their power.

The development of military facilities in Hawai'i brought many U.S. soldiers and sailors to the islands in the early 1900s.

Notable People

Many notable Hawai'ians have contributed to the development of their state and their country. These people include native Hawai'ians who led their country during challenging times. They also include a favorite son of Hawai'i who became the president of the United States and a religious leader who made ethical concerns a statewide issue. In addition, businesspeople and legislators have helped make Hawai'i the thriving, diverse state that it is today.

KAMEHAMEHA I (c.1758–1819)

According to Hawai'ian tradition, a bright star appeared in the sky just before King Kamehameha was born. Kamehameha united the islands in 1810 and maintained his people's independence through the early days of European and American exploration.

LILIUOKALANI (1838–1917)

Liliuokalani became queen of Hawai'i in 1891. She was greatly concerned about preserving Hawai'i for the Hawai'ians. American businessmen in Hawai'i opposed her rule. They overthrew her government in 1893. In 1895 she was forced to **abdicate** her throne. In 1898 Liliuokalani composed the song "Aloha Oe," much beloved in the islands.

FATHER DAMIEN (1840–1888)

Born in Belgium, Father Damien came to Hawai'i in 1864. When he heard that Hawai'ians who had contracted **leprosy** were being isolated on Molokai, he asked to be sent there to help them live and die with dignity. He knew that he too would probably get the disease. He died of leprosy in 1888, but his story brought much-needed help to the colony of lepers.

HIRAM L. FONG (1906–2004)

Hiram Fong was born in Honolulu in 1906, the seventh of eleven children in his Chinese American family. Fong was one of Hawai'i's first U.S. senators, serving from 1959 to 1977. He was the first Asian American to serve in the Senate.

BARACK OBAMA (1961–)

Barack Obama was born in Honolulu in 1961. He spent much of his youth in Hawai'i. After graduating from college and law school, Obama worked in Chicago, where he became involved in politics in the mid-1990s. He was a senator from Illinois when he decided to run for president. In 2008, Barack Obama was elected the 44th president of the United States. He is the first African American to serve in the office.

Duke Paoa Kahanamoku (1890–1968) was a native Hawai'ian surfer and swimmer in the early 1900s. He won three Olympic gold medals in swimming for the United States and is widely known for developing the flutter kick. He is considered one of the greatest freestyle swimmers of his time. Between 1932 and 1961, he served as the sheriff of the city and county of Honolulu.

George Ariyoshi (1926–), a Japanese American, was born in Honolulu and served in the state senate from 1959 to 1970. He served as governor of Hawai'i from 1973 to 1986. Ariyoshi was the first Japanese American governor of any U.S. state.

Population

H awai'i is the 40th most populous state in the Union. It is rich in ethnic variety. People have come from all over the world to make their homes on the islands. Fewer than 10 percent of the people living in Hawai'i today are descendants of the early Polynesians. The rest of Hawai'i's population represents a variety of ethnic origins, including people with ties to Japan, China, the Philippines, Korea, Thailand, Vietnam, and Portugal.

Although Oahu is not the largest of the islands, 75 percent of the state's residents live there. The rest of the residents are spread out among the other islands. The Big Island has the second-highest population, followed by Maui, Kauai, Molokai, and Lanai.

Hawai'i Population 1950–2010

Hawai'i's population has grown consistently since the middle of the 20th century. What are some reasons for the steady increase in population?

Number of People

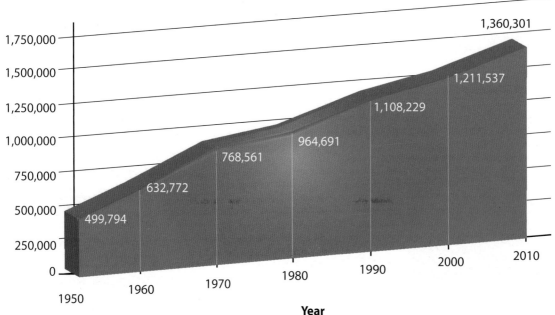

Children under the age of 18 make up more than 20 percent of Hawai'i's population.

More than one-third of the people of Hawai'i are Asian American.

Honolulu is the largest city in the state. The second largest is Hilo, on the island of Hawai'i.

Hawai'i is the most ethnically diverse state in the Union.

Over 900,000 people live in Honolulu County. More than 43 percent of them are of Asian descent.

Politics and Government

The structure of Hawai'i's local governments is different from any other state's. There are no municipal, or city, governments in Hawai'i. Instead, all local government functions are divided among four counties. The four main counties of the state are the County of Hawai'i; the County of Honolulu; the County of Kauai, which includes Kauai and Niihau; and the County of Maui, which includes Maui, Lanai, Kahoolawe, and nearly all of Molokai. A mayor and a council govern each county.

Iolani Palace served as the capitol building of the provisional government, republic, territory, and state of Hawai'i until 1969.

A fifth county in Hawai'i, the County of Kalawao, consists of the northern part of Molokai. This area is a settlement for people with leprosy. Because leprosy is an infectious disease, the state's Department of Health governs the County of Kalawao.

Hawai'i's state government is similar to that of other states. A governor and lieutenant governor head the executive branch. The two-house legislature is made up of a Senate, with 25 members, and a House of Representatives, with 51 members. Hawai'i's Supreme Court and lower courts make up the judicial branch.

Daniel Akaka is the first U.S. senator of native Hawai'ian ancestry. He has served as a senator from Hawai'i since 1991.

STATE OF HAWAII
1959
UA MAU KE EA O KA AINA I KA PONO

Hawai'i's state song is written in Hawai'ian. It is called "Hawai'i Ponoi," which means "Hawai'i's Own" in English.

Here is an excerpt from the song:

Hawai'i ponoi Nana i kou, moi Kalani Alii, ke Alii.
Makua lani e Kamehameha e Na kaua e pale Me ka i he.

translation:
Hawai'i's own true sons, be loyal to your chief
Your country's liege and lord, the Alii.
Father above us all, Kamehameha,
Who guarded in the war with his ihe.

Note: an ihe is a spear.

Cultural Groups

Hawai'ian society is a pleasant mix of cultures and customs. The various cultural groups living on the islands all contribute to the colorful life of the state. People in Hawai'i celebrate their distinctive cultures through their language, festivals, and food.

Hawai'ian and English are Hawai'i's two official languages. Almost everyone in Hawai'i speaks English. The Hawai'ian language, which originated with the early Polynesian settlers, is almost extinct. However, the language is still present in the names of places and in songs. People on the islands also use words from the Hawai'ian language in their everyday speech. English mixed with Hawai'ian is heard regularly. Other languages are also heard. Immigrants from China, Japan, and the Philippines often speak their native languages.

Chinese lion dancing has been popular in China for hundreds of years. Chinese Americans in Hawai'i celebrate their heritage by honoring their customs and participating in festivals.

One of Hawai'i's most famous customs is the traditional lei greeting. A lei is a wreath of flowers strung together and worn as a necklace. Visitors to the islands are often presented with a lei as a sign of welcome.

The Aloha Festival is celebrated on six Hawai'ian islands over a period of several months. It was created to honor Hawai'ian heritage and celebrate the aloha spirit.

In Hawai'i it is customary to remove your shoes before entering someone's home. This tradition stems from Japanese culture.

There are only 12 letters in the Hawai'ian alphabet. These letters are *a, e, h, i, k, l, m, n, o, p, u, w.*

Every August 21, Hawai'i celebrates Admission Day, which is the anniversary of its statehood.

June 11 is Kamehameha Day. On this day Hawai'ians honor the man who united their islands.

The Apology Bill, signed by President Bill Clinton in 1993, apologized to native Hawai'ians for the role of the United States government in the unlawful overthrow of the Hawai'ian government a century earlier.

Hawai'i's many festivals and events celebrate its diverse culture. Hawai'ians observe Chinese New Year, which falls in January or February. Japanese **bon dances** are performed in July or August to honor dead ancestors.

Festivals honoring Filipino culture are also celebrated. In the fall the Aloha Festival celebrates Hawai'ian culture with parades, races, dancing, and huge feasts.

Arts and Entertainment

Hawai'i has many foods that are unique to the state. All of these foods can be found at a traditional feast called a luau. The main feature of the luau is a whole roasted pig called a kalua pig. The pig is roasted in a huge pit called an imu. Poi is also served at a luau. Poi is a starchy paste made from the root of a taro plant. Traditionally, people do not eat poi with utensils. They scoop it out of a bowl with their fingers. Another type of food typically found at a luau is laulau. Laulau is pork, fish, or chicken wrapped with other ingredients in the leaves of the ti plant.

Hawai'ians celebrate good times with a feast called a luau. Traditionally they would thank the gods for their good luck at the luau.

Food is not the only feature of a luau. There is usually traditional dancing and music as well. Hula dancing is the most famous type of dancing on the islands. Hula dancers move their hips and arms gracefully. Their movements reveal a story or describe the beauty of the islands.

The dancers move to the music of the Hawai'ian guitar and the **ukulele**, among other instruments. The ukulele was adapted from a small guitar brought to the islands by Portuguese workers in the late 1800s. The Hawai'ian guitar, which was developed in Hawai'i around 1895, is a steel guitar. Both instruments are important to Hawai'ian music.

Hawai'ians have a great appreciation for art and promote all forms of it in the state. The Honolulu Academy of Arts museum has a large collection of Western art. The Bishop Museum, also in Honolulu, is dedicated to the study and conservation of the history and culture of the Pacific and its people. The museum's displays include archaeological discoveries, fish, shells, and plants from the Pacific islands.

Academy-Award-winning actress Nicole Kidman was born in Honolulu. She has been a Goodwill Ambassador for the United Nations Development Fund for Women since 2006.

I DIDN'T KNOW THAT!

In 1883 a sculptor named Thomas Gould presented Hawai'i with a statue of King Kamehameha I. The statue now stands near Kamehameha's birthplace on the island of Hawai'i.

Luaus usually last about 3 hours. They are typically held at sunset.

Singer and actress Bette Midler was born in Honolulu in 1945.

The island of Kauai was featured in Steven Spielberg's film *Jurassic Park*.

Sports

Hawai'i is a tropical playground. Its mild climate encourages locals and tourists to take part in many outdoor sports and recreational events. Golf courses and tennis courts are regular features throughout the islands. Some of the most beautiful golf courses in the world are in Hawai'i.

There are scenic bicycle paths and hiking trails on all the islands. Hikers and cyclists can explore the massive volcanoes, lush rain forests, and green valleys of Hawai'i. Guided nature walks and **ecotours** are also popular. Hawai'ian people are proud of their land and will happily share its beauty with anyone who wishes to honor it.

Michelle Wie, a Korean American born in Honolulu, began playing golf at the age of four. At age 11, she was the youngest player to qualify for a USGA amateur golf championship. She has won several championships since becoming a professional in 2009.

The islands are excellent for water sports. Scuba diving and snorkeling are very popular pastimes. Hawai'i's underwater scenery is spectacular. Not only do divers get to swim among colorful fish, but they also get to see amazing natural architecture. During the formation of the islands millions of years ago, molten lava spilled into the sea and cooled to form incredible structures. Deep in the ocean are huge cavelike rooms, archways, and tunnels, all made from lava.

Surfing originated in ancient Hawai'i and is now practiced at some 1,600 recognized surf spots throughout the islands. Surfers from all over the world come to Hawai'i to ride the waves. Beginners can take surfing lessons on Waikiki Beach.

The steady wind and surf conditions in Hawai'i have helped to make it one of the best windsurfing spots in the world. International windsurfing competitions are often held in Oahu.

Hawai'i surfing waves have two distinct seasons. The biggest waves hit the north shores of all the islands between November and March. In the summertime, however, the south shores of the islands get the better waves.

National Averages Comparison

The United States is a federal republic, consisting of fifty states and the District of Columbia. Alaska and Hawai'i are the only non-contiguous, or non-touching, states in the nation. Today, the United States of America is the third-largest country in the world in population. The United States Census Bureau takes a census, or count of all the people, every ten years. It also regularly collects other kinds of data about the population and the economy. How does Hawai'i compare to the national average?

Comparison Chart

United States 2010 Census Data *	USA	Hawai'i
Admission to Union	NA	August 21, 1959
Land Area (in square miles)	3,537,438.44	6,422.62
Population Total	308,745,538	1,360,301
Population Density (people per square mile)	87.28	211.80
Population Percentage Change (April 1, 2000, to April 1, 2010)	9.7%	12.3%
White Persons (percent)	72.4%	24.7%
Black Persons (percent)	12.6%	1.6%
American Indian and Alaska Native Persons (percent)	0.9%	0.3%
Asian Persons (percent)	4.8%	38.6%
Native Hawaiian and Other Pacific Islander Persons (percent)	0.2%	10.0%
Some Other Race (percent)	6.2%	1.2%
Persons Reporting Two or More Races (percent)	2.9%	23.6%
Persons of Hispanic or Latino Origin (percent)	16.3%	8.9%
Not of Hispanic or Latino Origin (percent)	83.7%	91.1%
Median Household Income	$52,029	$66,701
Percentage of People Age 25 or Over Who Have Graduated from High School	80.4%	84.6%

*All figures are based on the 2010 United States Census, with the exception of the last two items.

How to Improve My Community

Strong communities make strong states. Think about what features are important in your community. What do you value? Education? Health? Forests? Safety? Beautiful spaces? Government works to help citizens create ideal living conditions that are fair to all by providing services in communities. Consider what changes you could make in your community. How would they improve your state as a whole? Using this concept web as a guide, write a report that outlines the features you think are most important in your community and what improvements could be made. A strong state needs strong communities.

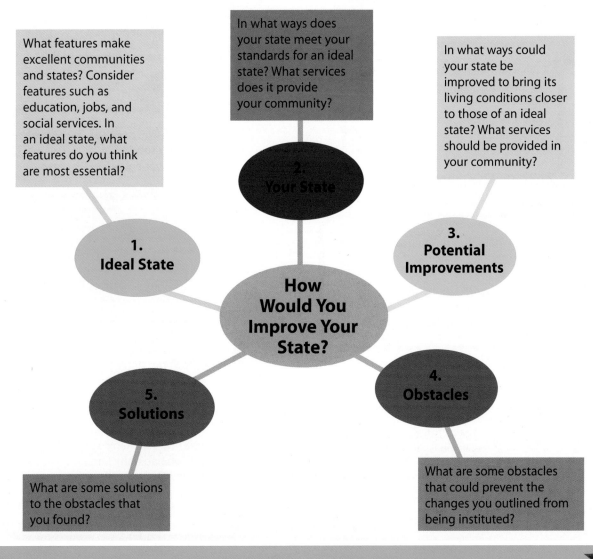

What features make excellent communities and states? Consider features such as education, jobs, and social services. In an ideal state, what features do you think are most essential?

In what ways does your state meet your standards for an ideal state? What services does it provide your community?

In what ways could your state be improved to bring its living conditions closer to those of an ideal state? What services should be provided in your community?

2. Your State

1. Ideal State

3. Potential Improvements

How Would You Improve Your State?

5. Solutions

4. Obstacles

What are some solutions to the obstacles that you found?

What are some obstacles that could prevent the changes you outlined from being instituted?

Exercise Your Mind!

Think about these questions and then use your research skills to find the answers and learn more fascinating facts about Hawai'i. A teacher, librarian, or parent may be able to help you locate the best sources to use in your research.

1 Which is the oldest of the Hawai'ian Islands?

a. Hawai'i
b. Kauai
c. Oahu

2 What kind of musical instrument is called the leaping flea?

a. the accordion
b. the kazoo
c. the ukulele

3 What famous American aviator is buried in Maui?

a. Charles Lindbergh
b. Amelia Earhart
c. Orville Wright

4 True or False? Hawai'i's Mauna Kea volcano is taller than Mt. Everest.

5 True or False? There are no more Hawai'ian Islands developing.

6 True or False? More than a quarter of all Hawai'ians speak a language other than English at home.

7 True or False? The Kilauea eruption of 1983 has not yet ended.

8 Here is a list of Hawai'ian words. See if you can find a pattern in the arrangement of letters.
hale (hah lay): house
huhu (hoo hoo): angry
kane (kah neh): man
moana (moh ah nah): ocean
ohana (oh hah nah): family
wahine (wah hee nay): woman
Did you notice anything special about the formation of these words?

Words to Know

abdicate: to give up one's throne

bon dances: Japanese Buddhist festival held to honor the dead

ecotours: tours to places that have unspoiled natural beauty

endangered: referring to a type of plant or animal that is at risk of disappearing from Earth

erosion: the process of slowly wearing away

geothermal: referring to using heat from within the Earth to produce electricity or other forms of energy

immunities: ability to fight infections and diseases

islets: small islands

leprosy: a contagious disease

monarchy: a form of government in which ultimate authority rests with a single person, such as a king or queen

patron: a person who gives financial or other kinds of help to another person

sandalwood: a fragrant wood used for carvings and burned as incense

taro: a tropical plant that can be eaten

threatened: referring to a type of plant or animal that is likely to become endangered, or at risk of disappearing from Earth

trade winds: very steady winds that produce fairly clear skies

ukulele: a small, guitarlike musical instrument

viable: practical or workable

Index

Log on to www.av2books.com

AV² by Weigl brings you media enhanced books that support active learning. Go to www.av2books.com, and enter the special code found on page 2 of this book. You will gain access to enriched and enhanced content that supplements and complements this book. Content includes video, audio, web links, quizzes, a slide show, and activities.

Audio
Listen to sections of
the book read aloud.

Video
Watch informative video clips.

Embedded Weblinks
Gain additional information
for research.

Try This!
Complete activities and
hands-on experiments.

WHAT'S ONLINE?

Try This!	Embedded Weblinks	Video	EXTRA FEATURES
Test your knowledge of the state in a mapping activity.	Discover more attractions in Hawai'i.	Watch a video introduction to Hawai'i.	**Audio** Listen to sections of the book read aloud.
Find out more about precipitation in your city.	Learn more about the history of the state.	Watch a video about the features of the state.	**Key Words** Study vocabulary, and complete a matching word activity.
Plan what attractions you would like to visit in the state.	Learn the full lyrics of the state song.		
Learn more about the early natural resources of the state.			**Slide Show** View images and captions, and prepare a presentation.
Write a biography about a notable resident of Hawai'i.			
Complete an educational census activity.			**Quizzes** Test your knowledge.

AV² was built to bridge the gap between print and digital. We encourage you to tell us what you like and what you want to see in the future.

Sign up to be an AV² Ambassador at www.av2books.com/ambassador.